and it has no beginning and it has no end day has no end night has no beginning and it has no beginning and it has no end day has no end night has no beginning and it has no beginning and it has no end day has no end night has no beginning and it has no beginning and it has no end day has no end night has no beginning

RUTH KRAUSS

Somebody Spilled the Sky

illustrated by
Eleanor Hazard

Greenwillow Books
A Division of
William Morrow & Company, Inc.
New York

Designed by Ava Weiss

First Edition

10 9 8 7 6 5 4 3 2 1

Library of Congress
Cataloging in Publication Data
Krauss, Ruth.
Somebody spilled the sky.
Summary: Sixteen poems of feelings,
thoughts, and behavior of childhood.
[1. American poetry]   I. Hazard,
Eleanor Lanahan.   II. Title.
PZ8.3.K865So   811'.5'4   78-14306
ISBN 0-688-80186-2
ISBN 0-688-84186-4 lib. bdg.

Contents

littlekid opera
BOW WOW WOW

Bow wow wow
Bow wow wow
Bow wow wow

repeat repeat

clap your hands
stamp your feet
skip all around to
the bow wow beat

CHORUS

Bow wow wow

Bow wow wow

Bow wow wow

repeat repeat

Duet

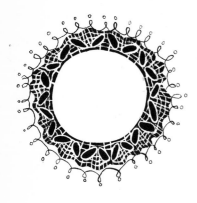

the day is so pretty

the umbrella is yellow

the day is so pretty
the sun is so shining

the umbrella is yellow
with white lace all around

the day is so yellow
the umbrella is so pretty
the sun is so all around
with white lace so shining

the umbrella is so yella
the sun is so pretty
with white all so shining
around lace so yellow umbrellow
with day is so yello sa yella
umbrella sa pretty sa yad

sa pretty sa yaddy
sa leylow sow lamu
brell white lace with shining
the sun is so all around

the day is so pretty
the umbrella is yellow
the day is so pretty
the sun is so shining
the umbrella is yellow
with white lace all around

When First I Saw

When first I saw the loud young land
I threw my arms around my world
and when I saw the small black lambs wandering in the red poppies
I threw my arms around my world and
loved it

Where

Where does that river come from
It comes from the mountain
Where does the mountain come from
It comes out of the world
Where does the world come from
It comes from the sun
Where does that sun come from
It comes from
It comes

Bell

BELL: begins ringing

CHILD: Mama Mama,
is that the bell for springtime?

MOTHER: No, silly, that's the door bell.
Would you answer it please.

DIRECTIONS: CHILD runs to the door

CHILD: Mama Mama, it's a man with the sun.

MOTHER: Well, dear, tell him to leave it.

CHILD: He says it's C.O.D.
And Mama, it's all tied up in ribbons and moths.

MOTHER: Ask him to bring it back tomorrow please.
We have no money in the house.

CHILD: Mama, he should leave it anyway.
It was the bell for springtime
and if we don't take it in but
send it away—
Mother Mother, the sun—
what will happen to it?

MOTHER: Well, I don't know.
Shells are full of the sea
the sea is full of waterbabies
and if you look in the eyes of the waterbabies...

. . . .

Tell the man to take away the sun
and bring you a waterbaby.

CHILD: Sir, we have no money for the C.O.D.
Could you please leave the sun
and it shine anyway?

MAN: Why not.
Here.

DIRECTIONS: CHILD takes the sun
and does a sun dance

Song and Act

When I see a field
I go crazy like a horse

When I see a worker
I go crazy like a boss

When I see a moon
I go crazy like a tide

the world is wide
O wide

When I see a chair
I go crazy like a table

When I see a horse
I go crazy like a stable

When I see a carousel
I go crazy like a ride

The world is wide
O wide

15

'b' Ballet

be a crumb hiding under the pillows

be a button   they push you and the moon comes on

be a seashell
roaring back
at the thruway

be the world and you turn keeping time with a clock
("With the minute hand?")

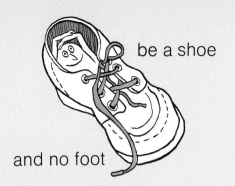

be a shoe

and no foot

be gum
stuck under tables
in restaurants

be a road and you go

be a ride - around - the- world without holding

be knock - on -your - head

be   who's there

buy a yellow hat to match the sun

Opera

"If you are the East Wind
I will be the rain"

"I am the East Wind"
"I am the rain"

**"If you are the springtime
I will be a cherry tree"**

"I am the springtime"
"I am a cherry tree"

"east wind"
"rain"
"springtime"
"cherry tree"

"springtime"
"cherry tree"
"east wind"
"rain"

"east **tree cherry** rain springtime wind
springtime rain **tree cherry** wind east"
*la la la la la la
la la la la la*

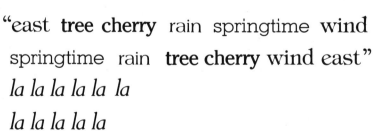

A Girl at a Party

There was a girl at a party
and she was very beautiful.
Her face was beautiful.
Her dress was beautiful.
Her feet were beautiful.
Everybody said, "How beautiful!"
And she was rich too.
But the other girls at the party didn't care
because they all had warm bathrobes.

A Beautiful Day

GIRL: What a beautiful day!

THE SUN falls down onto the stage

Weather

Drizzle tonight off the east coast of my head

snow melting
broken shore
little pine tree

26

Ten Nos *

NO
NO
NO
NO

NO
NO
NO
NO

NO
NO
NO
NO

NO
NO

*sonnet

DO NOT OPEN UNTIL BIRTHDAY

beginning on paper

on paper
I write it
on rain

I write it
on stones
on my boots

on trees
I write it
on the air

on the city
how pretty
I write my name

O! SOMEBODY spilled the sky